269 Facts For Adults

FUNNY, CRAZY, & UNBELIEVABLE FACTS
THAT'LL BLOW YOUR MIND

TABLE OF CONTENTS

269 FACTS

1.   Among   scientists,   there   is   a   popular evolutionary theory about the reason why the end of the human male's penis is mushroom shaped, which claims that it's required to scrape other men's ejaculate from the female's vagina.

2. An American survey with 27,000 participants has established that the percentage of people in their early twenties who said they had no sexual partner after turning eighteen increased from 6% in the 1960's, to 15% in the 1990's. The difference is mostly a result of the cohort effect, which means that sexual behavior seems to have changed in between the age groups.

3. When men turn seventy, they are still sexually vigorous. Research has shown that around 73% of older men are still potent.

4. In 1996, a study revealed that there is no perceptible difference in the vagina size of a woman who has or has not given birth.

5. Ginger is an aphrodisiac. It will increase your heart rate, get blood flowing through your veins and get you ready for the night ahead. Other foods   with   similar   propertics   include blackberries, oysters and watermelon.

6. During an orgasm or arousal, the endorphins released by the body bring a feeling that is similar to the one you experience with opioid drugs.

7. By pure flexibility, one in a thousand men are said to be able to orally please themselves and no rib removal is actually required.

8. Inside a man's sperm there are certain proteins that can actually act as a natural skin-tightening agent and moisturizer, which means that sperms can be highly effective at treating wrinkles. Its active ingredients are vitamins B12, C, and E, and it even contains essential minerals like magnesium, calcium, zinc, phosphor, and potassium. On average there are only two to five milliliters of semen which contains anywhere from forty million to half a billion sperm. It can also give you a beautiful smile as the zinc and calcium help fight off tooth decay.

9. According to studies, almost 50% of all men think that their penis is too small.

10. In Italy, the name of the movie "Moana" was changed to "Oceana" by Disney because Moana Posey is the name of a famous Italian porn star there. Although she passed away in 1994, her name is still remembered and linked to the porn business.

1. One out of every ten European babies is conceived on an IKEA bed.

2. In 2010, a study concluded that men who have sex at least twice a week can actually reduce their risk of heart disease by nearly 50%.

13. After Carrie Fisher's screenwriter friend Heather Robinson got sexually harassed by a producer, the actress went to the guy's house, and hand delivered a package, along with a note. The package had a cow's tongue in it, and the note said that if the man ever touched Heather again, or any other lady for that matter, the next package would contain something that belonged to the guy, in a tinier box.

14. Most condoms now are made with latex or Polyurethane which are better at protecting against Sexually Transmitted Infections (STIs). Animal skin condoms aren't as retentive and secure, sometimes allowing the passage of viruses including HIV.

15. Women who have sex at least once a week have more regular menstrual cycles.

16. Prostitutes in ancient Greece used to wear sandals that left the words "follow me" imprinted in the dirt as they walked. That was their way to advertise their services.

.7. The most common places where people have sex are their own bedrooms, the bathtub, shower, n the car, or in one of their child's bedrooms.

18. On average, red-headed women have more sex and even more orgasms than ladies with any other hair color.

19. Approximately 16% of all sexually active women claim that they have never had an orgasm during intercourse. In fact, some women have never had one at all.

20. The longer a man waits to have sex again, the lower his sperm count is according to research. If a man has daily sex, not only will he have more sperm, but the quality of it will be superior, which makes him more fertile.

21. Different studies have shown that those people who are into kinkier sex positions and open to being tied up or dominated during sex are psychologically healthier than traditional performers.

22. The first vibrator was actually invented in 1890. It looked more like a kitchen mixer than a sex toy and it was powered by a hand-crank. The device was marketed as a way to reduce hysteria in women. Today over 61% of women find the idea of buying a sex toy arousing in and of itself.

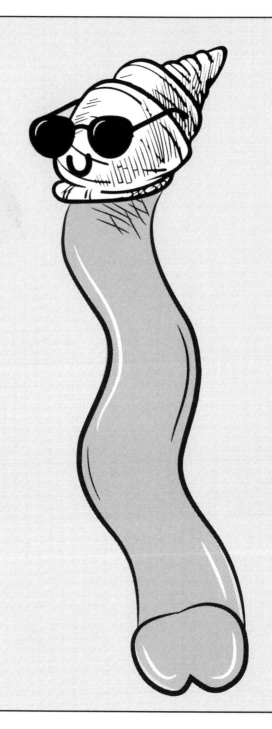

23. The creature with the largest penis in relation to its body is the barnacle. Its penis can be nearly forty times the length of its own body.

24. It has been scientifically proven that sex helps to reduce stress and a person's blood pressure by releasing oxytocin into the body during an orgasm, calming nerves. This is because oxytocin counteracts the cortisol's hormone effects released under stress.

25. Back in 2009, a twenty eight year old Russian man named Sergey Tuganow accepted a wager with two ladies that they'd pay him 3,000 pounds if he could have sex with them for twelve hours straight. He managed the feat half a day later with the help of a bottle of Viagra, and soon after collecting his 3,000 pounds, he suffered a heart attack and dropped dead.

26. It's considered unfashionable for men to wear green hats in China because it indicates that a man has been cheated on by his wife. This started way back in the Yuan Dynasty, when people were made to wear green headwear as a sign of shame, or if they had a prostitute for a family member.

27. A person's pain threshold increases considerably during arousal, meaning more vigorous and playful sex.

28. The chimaera, or ghost shark, lives in the darkest parts of the ocean where the sun can't reach. They don't have teeth, are dead-eyed, and the males have a retractable sex organ on their foreheads. These deep-sea creatures split-off from other groups, some 300 million years ago, and are relatives of sharks and rays.

29. In Guelph, Ontario, there is a strip club that also serves as a church. On Sunday mornings, Sharon and Jack Ninaber work together with some volunteers to turn "The Manor" – which is the name of the strip club – into a church, hold a service, and afterwards, they rearrange the place, turning it back into a strip club.

30. Orgasms in men usually last anywhere from six to nine seconds, while in women they often last for more than twenty seconds, with some exceptions lasting for a few minutes.

31. There is a condition called "diphallus" where one in every five million people is born with two penises. Besides having the condition, it has also been documented only a handful of times that they are able to use both for intercourse.

32. The "Erection Hardness Scale" is an actual system that's used to measure erections. It was devised by researchers in the 1990's who needed a way to test Viagra.

33. The only members of the primate family that don't have bones in their penises are human males. According to scientists, this can be an evolutionary trait.

34. Southern California removed "Tenth Edition Merriam Webster Dictionaries" from fourth and fifth grade classrooms in 2010 because they had an entry that defined oral sex.

35. In Soviet labor camps, people would sneak out, swallow condoms that were linked to rubber tubes, fill the condoms with concentrated raw alcohol, and then sneak back in. Other detainees would hold them in the upside down position so that they could be used as human kegs.

36. When mating, the male sea otter grips his teeth onto the females' nose. That is why the females get the nickname Rudolph during the reproduction cycle, as their noses are red after mating.

37. At some point during sex, 20% of all sexually active people between the ages of eighteen and thirty four use their smartphone.

38. During intense sex, an erect penis can actually break, by twisting or crushing after slipping out, which can burst blood vessels and cause swelling.

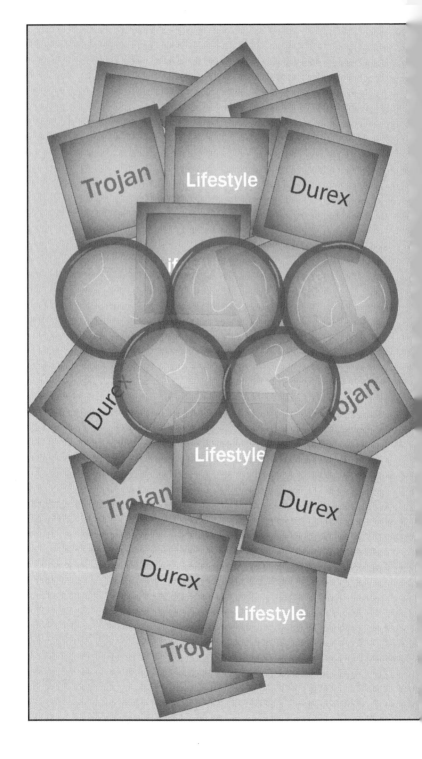

CONDOM FACTS

39. The most popular condom brand in the US is Trojan.

40. Condoms have been used since 3000 B.C.

41. During the 2018 Winter Olympics, 110,000 condoms were distributed to Athletes.

42. On Valentine's Day, eighty seven condoms are used every second.

43. A regular condom can hold a gallon (3.8 liters) of water.

44. Condoms lose their integrity over time and can deteriorate so it's important to look at the expiration date before use. Changes in temperature from hot to cold and excess rubbing (keeping a condom in your wallet) cause them to deteriorate quicker. It's recommended to keep them in a dry, cool place where there is no risk of them getting bent.

45. Less than 40% of students are taught how to put a condom on in Health Class in High School.

46. One in four acts of vaginal intercourse is condom-protected in the US.

47. The fear of seeing, thinking about, or having an erect penis is called "ithyphallophobia." The origin of the word "ithy" is Greek and means straight, "phallo" in Greek means penis, and "phobia" in Greek means fear.

48. In the states of Alabama and Mississippi, sex toys and vibrators are banned in shops. According to the Attorney General, there is no fundamental right for a person to buy a device to produce an orgasm.

49. Based on studies conducted by researchers from Israel and Australia, a small concentration of Viagra dissolved in a base of water can double the shelf life of flowers, making them stand up straight for as long as a week beyond their natural life span.

50. Between 2002 and 2010, zipper mishaps caused nearly 18,000 men to end up at ER. That is almost one fifth of all penis injuries during this time.

51. Sexually frustrated young male dolphins have been known to go on murder rampages, killing single or multiple other porpoises.

52. In 2014, a study revealed that lesbians tend to have more orgasms when compared to heterosexual and bisexual women.

53. An experiment was performed by the show Mythbusters to see if large breasted servers made more money in tips. They found that men tipped large breasted servers 30% more, but even more strangely, women tipped them 40% more.

54. By the end of your life, odds are you will have spent more than 20,000 minutes kissing. That translates to two weeks of your life with your lips locked with someone else's.

55. During World War II, itching powder was placed into condoms by Britain's special operations executives. They were intended for use by German servicemen stationed in Norway.

56. Hiring strippers to perform at funerals was a common practice in rural China in order to attract mourners. The practice was banned in 2015.

57. Endangered great apes known as bonobos are the last remaining closest relatives to humans. They are bisexual by nature, and where sex is concerned, they don't seem to discriminate on the basis of gender or age.

58. 46% of people in the US think there's more of a chance of them seeing Bigfoot than the chance of them cumming at the same time their partner will.

59. Netflix has come up with a Netflix and chill button called "The Switch." When you press it, "The Switch" dims the lights, activates your phone's do-not-disturb feature, and gets Netflix ready for streaming.

60. "Seduction of the Innocent" is a book written by psychologist Fredric Wertham in the 1950's. In the book, Batman and Robin are accused of being homosexual, and Superman of being a fascist right-wing fantasy.

61. In the eighteenth and nineteenth centuries, there was a popular hot drink called "saloop" that was a cheaper alternative to tea and coffee. However, rumors started spreading that the drink cured venereal diseases, and it became shameful to be seen drinking it, so it was removed from shops.

62. Five Americans have accidentally shot their penis off since 2010.

63. In 2002, a former intern at NASA named Thad Roberts was sent to prison for six years after stealing moon rocks gathered from the Apollo 11 moon landing mission. He stole the rocks to have sex with his girlfriend on them.

64. Throughout its history, the NBA has never had a player who wore jersey number sixty nine.

65. In the insect world, sexual cannibalism is actually a common event. It occurs when one partner, typically the female, eats the other after mating. This is the reason why praying mantis males, for example, become motionless after mating, to avoid being eaten.

66. When a woman experiences an orgasm, an endorphin is released into the woman's body that can actually alleviate pain.

67. On average, women in their twenties are more likely to have only one orgasm per sexual encounter. In contrast, women over the age of forty tend to have multiple orgasms.

68. A "merkin" is a type of wig for a person's private area. It was invented in the 1400's and women who had shaven their pubic hair in fear of lice wore it.

69. In Dildo, a town in Newfoundland, residents believe that it's the happiest place in the world. They celebrate Dildo Day over there and they have an official mascot: a fisherman called "Captain Dildo."

70. For every thirty minutes of sex, an adult human burns on average over 200 calories. The number can be higher depending on the sex position and how vigorous the intercourse is.

71. Roman Emperor Claudius' third wife, Valeria Messalina, reportedly liked to moonlight as a sex worker. It was said that she once competed with a local prostitute to see who could bed more men within a night, and the empress actually won.

72. Doctors working at Tulane University in the fifties discovered how to use electrodes to trigger the pain and pleasure centers in the brain. In a well-known experiment, they gave a female subject an orgasm that lasted thirty minutes.

73. In the past, blowing smoke up your ass was actually a common cure for many ailments.

74. Honey bees can actually infect each other with diseases through sexual activities, and because the queen mates with hundreds of male bees in just a few hours, the STD can spread in the hive extremely fast.

75. In 2012, 55,000 condoms with QR tracking codes on them were given away by Planned Parenthood of the Greater Northwest to students at Western Washington colleges. The students could scan the codes and answer detailed questions about the place you had sex, if you used a condom, how it was, etc. It then puts a pin on the map and asks if you want to share it to Facebook and Twitter.

76. Depending on the state of the man it comes from, only 1-10% of his semen is sperm. In every teaspoon of semen, there are more than 300 million sperm within the average healthy human male. Depending on the source, that teaspoon would contain around one calorie if consumed.

77. Truvada is a type of drug that has been shown to prevent HIV infection at a 92% success rate for gay men, and a 70% success rate for intravenous drug users. However, less than 1% of at-risk people currently take the drug, and only 1/3 of primary care doctors have even heard of it.

78. Women experience a reduction in their amygdala and hippocampus when having an orgasm. Those are the parts of the brain that allow them to feel anxiety and fear. In other words, women feel less anxious and afraid after sex.

79. In March of 2015, a poll taken about women's health and happiness revealed that almost 62% of women are not satisfied with their sex lives. However, 85% of them claimed to be fine with their partner's penis length.

80. Sylvester Graham, a Presbyterian minister, was the first to invent the Graham cracker as a method to help curb sexual desire.

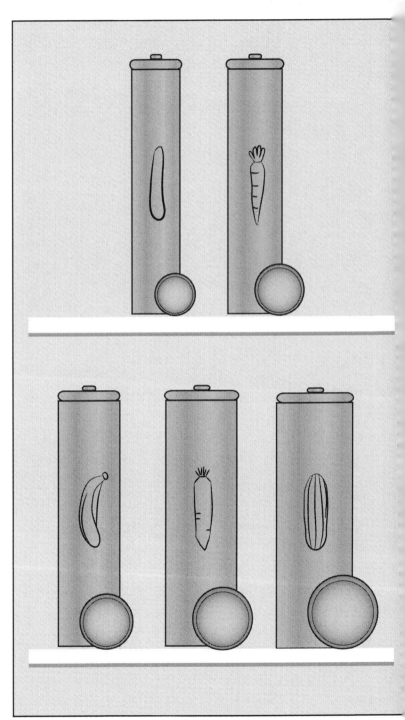

81. "Love Guide" is a condom packaging system developed by Taiwanese student Guan Hao Pan for people who always buy the wrong size. The packaging comes in five different shapes and sizes, including zucchini, carrot, banana, turnip, and cucumber.

82. According to research, when having sex with a man with a penis that is circumcised or uncircumcised, there is little to no difference in feeling for women.

83. In Paraguay's Ache tribe, babies have multiple dads, and they include all the men who slept with the baby's mother at the time of pregnancy. After birth, the babies are cared for by all those men, who help feed and raise them.

84. Nintendo used to operate "love hotels" in Japan in the sixties. These hotels charged hourly rates and guests were mostly sex workers and couples.

85. A study done in 2012 showed that the average ejaculation duration of a high performance boar was six minutes. They even reported one boar that orgasmed continuously for thirty one minutes.

86. Putting salt on your tongue has been shown to reduce the gag reflex in some people.

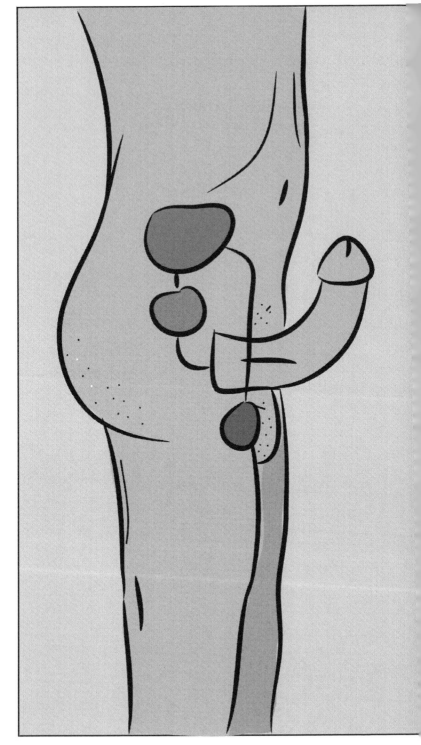

37. Peyronie's disease is a condition presented in one in four men. It's when their penis is bent slightly more than normal when erect. Some men require surgery to enjoy pain-free sex while others only need to find a comfortable position.

38. Being aroused and having an orgasm can actually boost your immune system, hence making you healthier.

89. "La petite mort," or "the little death" in English, is what the French call an orgasm. The reason why that is because it's believed that your soul temporarily goes to another place after you have given all you have to experience joy.

90. The "Fellowship of the Naked Trust" is the first nudist colony in the world and it was pioneered in 1891 in India.

91. Prostitutes in ancient China drank an herbal concoction called "liangyao" that contained musk which worked as a contraception. It actually worked by causing sterility.

92. According to a study done in May of 2013, 54% of the 2,346 professionals surveyed admitted to have had sex with a work colleague at least once in their lives. In addition, 12% of adults admitted to having had a sexual encounter at least once in the workplace.

CONDOM FACTS PART II

93. The average shelf life of a latex condom is three to five years.

94. To avoid the use of humans and animals, condom companies send electric currents through condoms to check for any holes in them. Each individual condom has an electrical conductance test done on it before it's sold. The condom should block the flow of electricity and if it's intact i.e. no tears and rips, then it will be able to properly insulate the electricity.

95. The first condoms were made from sheep intestines.

96. Over 450 million condoms are sold each year in the United States alone.

97. The first rubber condom was made in 1855.

98. The first televised advertisement for a condom was in 1975 by the condom company Trojan.

99. The German Military was the first to promote condom use among its soldiers. They were also the biggest exporters to Europe and Australia.

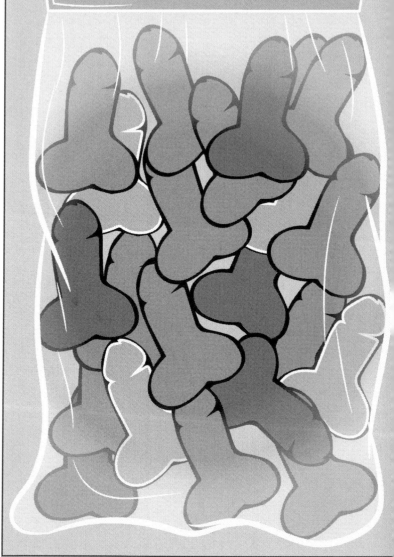

100. Originally, the melody used in America's national anthem, "The Star Spangled Banner," belonged to a British song called "Anacreon in Heaven," which was about drinking and sex.

101. The only other documented species that have sex for pleasure and not just for procreation are dolphins.

102. It has been proven that taking the time to cuddle after sex helps increase both parties' overall enjoyment of the encounter.

103. An English man was sick and tired that his city wasn't repairing potholes so he painted penises on them with spray paint. He was later nicknamed as "Wanksy."

104. DicksByMail.com is a company that, for $15, mails a five ounce (141 gram) bag of gummy bear dicks, with a letter that reads: "Eat a Bag of Dicks." The bag can be mailed to anyone you want.

105. The blue whale is the animal with the largest recorded functioning penis in the world; it measures over ten feet (three meters) long.

106. Hugging for thirty seconds is a quick way to get into the mood. It increases the oxytocin hormone as well as libido.

107. The impulse to ejaculate comes from the spinal cord and no brain is needed. Men and women can still orgasm after a spinal cord injury, and cases have even been recorded of people reaching climax after death.

108. People can have orgasms even without any sexual stimulation. Women have stated they have had orgasms during gym workouts, doing yoga, and even whilst giving childbirth. Some women have claimed to experience one while horse riding, in front of a photocopier and even standing still and just thinking.

109. When it comes to who has longer orgasms, women take the crown. Women last twenty seconds, while men last ten to fifteen seconds on average. Pigs can have one that lasts thirty minutes.

110. A study found that 84% of women have sex just to get their partners to do more work around the house.

111. Approximately 5% of forty year old men and between 15-25% of sixty-five year old men experience erectile dysfunction.

112. Americans spend less than an hour per week having sex which is fourteen minutes below the global average.

113. Among sexually active American teens, over half of all males and 70% of females stated that their first sexual experience was with a long term partner.

114. The average person has sex a little over one hundred times per year.

115. Approximately one in ten married adults said that they normally sleep by themselves.

116. The average erect penis is four to six inches in circumference.

117. The average male loses his virginity just before his seventeenth birthday while females lose it slightly later, shortly after they turn seventeen years old.

118. A new study showed that genetic factors such as impulsivity can make a person more or less willing to have sex at an earlier age.

119. Approximately 30% of women in Britain think that they can avoid pregnancy by jumping up and down right after having sex.

120. Originally, Viagra was developed as a medication to treat high blood pressure issues. The fact that it enhances erections was discovered later purely by accident.

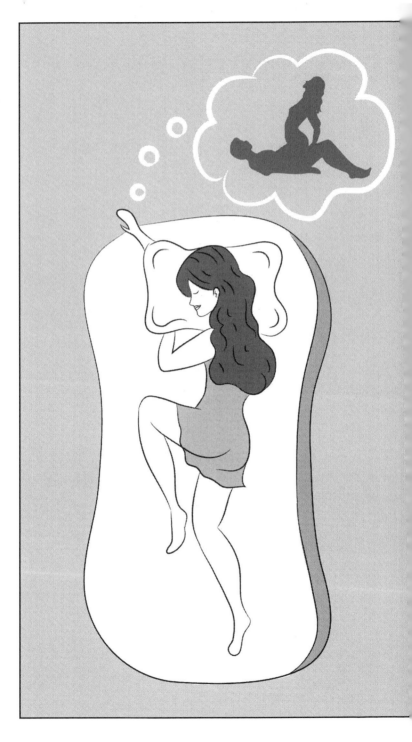

21. Women have the ability to have wet dreams as well. It usually occurs when they hit the rapid eye movement (REM) sleep cycle. This is usually after an hour and a half to two hours after you fall asleep and the vagina has increased blood flow.

122. Women have the ability to change their voices to sound sexier, however, when men do it, they are rated as sounding worse.

123. Research has shown that women on the pill have a different taste in men than if they weren't on it. Women on the pill were more attracted to men with less masculine physical characteristics and lower testosterone.

124. Love can make you obsessive. Scans done on an MRI have shown that falling in love can send a rush of blood to the pleasure center of your brain which is the same area that's responsible for compulsive and obsessive behaviors. Serotonin is also lowered when you are in love which is common with people who have compulsive-obsessive disorders.

125. Most condoms break because they are either too big or too small for the user.

126. The word pornographic comes from the Greek meaning "the writing of prostitutes."

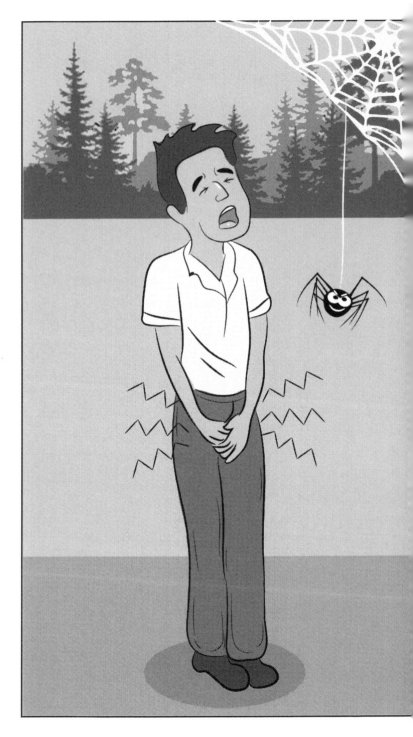

127. It's known that people who have narcissistic tendencies have sex for power, and not romance or love.

128. There is a spider in Brazil known as the "wandering spider" that is known to give its victims not only pain and increased blood pressure, but a painful boner after they've been bitten. Scientists are currently investigating the venom as a potential treatment for erectile dysfunction.

129. Some women are able to have an orgasm just from having their breasts stimulated.

130. A study performed at Wilkes University in Pennsylvania found that students in college who have sex two or more times a week get sick less often. This is because they have more antibodies of immunoglobulin in their system which boosts the immune system.

131. The longest kiss goes to a couple who set a record in 2005 for thirty one hours and thirty minutes.

132. Death during sex is more common than you might think. Some estimates claim that 0.6% of all sudden deaths occur during sexual intercourse. The most common root causes are cardiac episodes as well as brain hemorrhages.

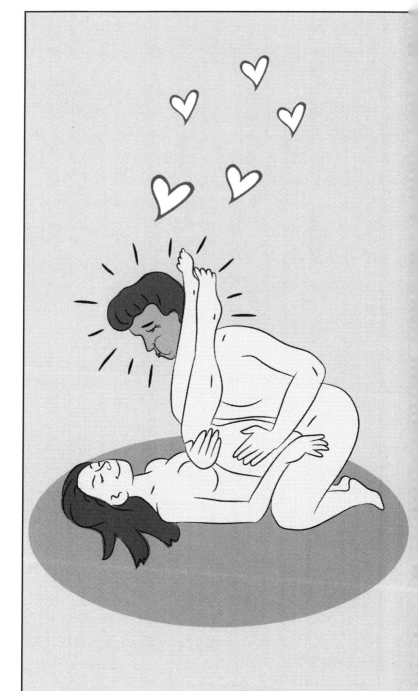

133. Having an orgasm is better for your brain than a session of Sudoku.

134. A university study found that couples who are having sex that is boring still makes them happier than couples who aren't doing it at all.

135. Studies have found that women wearing socks while in bed have a 30% more chance of climaxing than those without.

136. The most undiagnosed STI in the US is Chlamydia which is also the most common.

137. At least one in four people in the US - perhaps as many as one in two - will contract an STI at some point in their lives.

138. 44% of men say that bad sex in a relationship is a deal breaker, however, when women were asked the number was over 50%.

139. Some people have been known to lose their mind after sex. It's known as "transient amnesia" (short term temporary memory loss) and is caused by intense sex.

140. By holding your breath when having sex you let less oxygen go to your genitals and men can last longer. By breathing more you become more aroused and it feels better.

141. Some females breasts are able to swell up to 25% larger than their usual size when they are aroused. The top of the breast is usually the most sensitive while the bottom of the breast is the least sensitive.

142. Research shows that men who have sex within a relationship report greater pleasure than guys who have no-strings-attached sex.

143. The average speed of a guy's ejaculation is twenty seven miles per hour (forty five kilometers per hour).

144. A womens clitoris has approximately eight thousand nerve endings, some of which actually extend all the way up to where the pubic hair is. This is the reason why it still feels good for women when someone is rubbing/grinding up against it. The clitoris also continues to grow until the age of thirty, becoming four times its original size since puberty.

145. When some women's nipples are stimulated, the same part of their brain is activated as if someone were stimulating their clitoris or vagina.

146. If presented with these foods, many women would give up sex to have them. They are: chocolate, steak, and sushi.

147. Research shows that premature ejaculation is experienced more by men than erectile dysfunction. Ejaculating before two minutes is defined as premature and one in three men experience this phenomenon.

148. According to a survey, the most popular athletes to turn women on are footballers and swimmers.

149. Some of the most bizarre fetishes include autoplushophilia (arousal at oneself dressed as a giant, cartoon-like stuffed animal), autonepiophilia (arousal at oneself in the form of an infant), climacophilia (arousal at falling down stairs), and lithophilia (arousal at stone and gravel).

150. Some men are able to orgasm without ejaculating.

151. The average person with a penis will ejaculate fourteen gallons of semen over their lifetime. Most of that will be through masturbation.

152. Studies have shown that women who have sex without condoms are less depressed. Researchers believe this is due to the hormones in semen that are absorbed into the woman's body.

153. THE TOP TEN MOST POPULAR PUBLIC PLACES TO HAVE SEX ARE:

Public park, field, or garden
In a car
At the beach
In a public bathroom
In the cinemas
At university or in the library
Department store change room
Swimming pool
On a balcony
At work

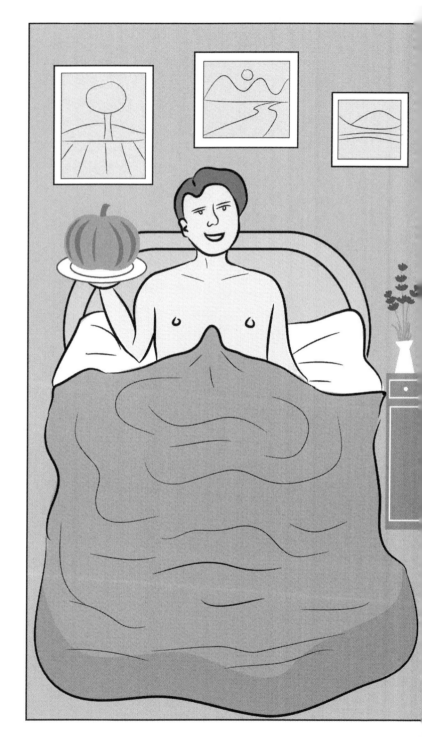

154. Research has found that the average women in college thinks about sex ten times throughout the day whereas a male college student will think about it for double that amount.

155. Over half the individuals who reported having sex between the ages of fifteen and nineteen wished they'd waited longer before their first time.

156. More than a quarter of women and a third of men over the age of fifty have given oral sex in the last year.

157. The smell of pumpkin and lavender can increase blood flow to the penis.

158. Research has shown that when you are sexually aroused your body temperature increases, hence, the reason why some people's chest and face become red during sex. The pinkish red rash disappears shortly after having sex.

159. Close to 90% of men said that their female partner had an orgasm in their most recent sexual encounter, however, when women were asked, the number stated was 60%.

160. The percentage for a woman climaxing increases as she gets older.

161. Almost half of all women would give up sex for two weeks rather than giving up the Internet for the same time period.

162. One in ten men say they have sex to help them relieve stress.

163. Some men break their penises on purpose. In a practice known as taqaandan ("to click" in Kurdish), men will hold the lower shaft of their erect penis with one hand then use the other to quickly snap the upper shaft. When done correctly, taqaandan is said to be painless.

164. 72% of women have stated that they have had a drunken one night stand that they don't remember.

165. When the human female's vagina is stimulated, it can expand to nearly twice its normal size.

166. Human papillomavirus (HPV), a virus that's transmitted by intercourse or oral sex, is present in over 60% of healthy Americans. There are two different types of HPV; high rish and low risk. Low risk HPV causes genital warts whereas high risk can cause different types of cancer. Usually, within two years the body's immune system is able to fight off the disease for up to 90% of people.

167. Sexual motivation varies individual to individual and the way your brain is wired may influence the number of sexual partners you have over the course of your lifetime. Individuals who showed more brain activity when they saw a sexualized image had more sexual partners.

168. Approximately 7% of adult women and 8% of adult males identify themselves as bisexual. However, the number of adults who have reported having had a same-sex experience in their lives is significantly higher.

169. You can burn two to three calories by making out passionately. The average couple burns 3.6 calories per minute of sexual intercourse.

170. Two out of every hundred men think that satisfying sex is a top priority in their lives and many others say that having sex regularly brings as much happiness as earning an extra six figures a year.

171. There is an 80% chance that a woman sleeping around without any contraceptive will become pregnant within twelve months.

172. Avocados are known as the "fruit of the testicle tree" and are believed to have aphrodisiac qualities.

173. According to a survey, the best lovers are found in Spain, Brazil, and Italy.

174. A third of men fantasize more about money than they do about sex.

175. Even though most women say they are straight, a study found that most women were aroused when they saw women's bodies, homosexual acts, and even animals having sex.

176. Close to 60% of all men are circumcised.

177. The act of watching relationship themed movies together with your partner reduces the chances of splitting up with them.

178. 28% of Americans are living with an incurable STD.

179. 67% of college students have engaged in a friends with benefits relationship. More than half who engaged in the relationship said they had all forms of sex, 22% said they only had sex while 8% said they did everything but have sex.

180. A third of people begin scrolling their phones right after having sex.

181. A woman's vagina narrows before having sex for a better grip on the penis.

182. Approximately 70% of American teenagers have had sex by the age of nineteen.

183. Candles are the most used things for females to have fun with after fingers and vibrators.

184. Penile rupture can occur due to vigorous masturbation. It happens when you're doing it wrong.

185. Some individuals have stated that they experience the same feelings of excitement when they think about food as when having sex.

186. The average vagina is three to four inches long but can expand by 200% when sexually aroused.

187. Despite what men say, only 15% have a package more than seven inches long while 3% have a penis longer than eight inches.

188. Orgasms can lower a woman's risk of heart disease, stroke, breast cancer, and depression.

189. A survey from Time Out New York found that guys are in on the trick too and almost 31% of guys have faked an orgasm.

190. Sex is ten times more effective than Valium.

191. When a kiss occurs, approximately ten million to one billion bacteria are exchanged.

192. Forty four year old Jonah Falcon holds the record for the largest penis with a package that measures 9.5 inches (twenty three centimeters) flaccid and 13.5 inches (thirty four centimeters) erect. He was once even stopped at an airport security screening as the officers suspected he was carrying something.

193. Sleep-deprived men are more likely to believe that women want to have sex with them.

194. A man's sperm can live for forty eight hours inside the female body, however, there have been documented cases of sperm living in there after eight days from having sex.

195. In the UK, 90% of adults admitted to having some form of sexual interaction in the office.

196. You can't say happiness without saying penis.

197. The Kama Sutra has over 250 references to different types of kisses, when to kiss, and how to kiss.

198. Shaving your pubic area increases your chances of spreading an STI.

199. Scientists are unsure why humans have pubic hair, but they theorize that the hair traps secretions that hold pheromones, or sexual scents.

200. During D-Day, thousands of condoms were given to soldiers. Most of them were used to keep their rifles dry.

201. The average length of an erect penis is from five to seven inches (12.7 to 17.7 centimeters), while a flaccid one is around 3.61 inches (9.1 centimeters).

202. Statistics show that approximately one in every five Americans has indulged in sex with a colleague at work.

203. Singles have worse sleep in general than those who are in stable relationships.

204. Almost half of all women consider it cheating when their partners are just fantasizing about someone else.

205. You're less likely to find someone or something disgusting if you're aroused.

206. Men who get married after the age of twenty five have stronger skeletons than men who get married before.

207. Polyorchidism is a very rare congenital condition where a male is born with more than two testicles.

208. 50% of all women have faked at least one orgasm in their lives. The number in Australia for Australian women is higher at 62%.

209. With the exception of the seventy and above age group, 60% of men have masturbated at least once in the last year while the number is 84% of men between the ages of twenty four and thirty. The numbers for women on the other hand are lower by up to 10-30% for the same age groups.

210. When golfers were asked if they would give up sex for a better swing, over 40% said they would.

211. A sperm takes one hour to swim seven inches.

212. Only 13% of American teens have had sex when they're fifteen, however by their nineteenth birthday, the number shoots up to 70%.

213. 52% of Americans aren't satisfied with their sex lives.

214. Four popes have died while having sex.

USEFUL TIPS

215. Individuals who are more open and comfortable talking about the topic of sex are more content with their sex lives than others.

216. Having too high a level of cholesterol in your diet can cause erectile dysfunction and it can act as a warning for cardiovascular disease.

217. You can experience a more intense orgasm if you tighten and squeeze your PC muscles for a few moments right before you climax.

218. The average length of foreplay between couples lasts between eleven and thirteen minutes. Lovers who spend twenty minutes or more on foreplay with their women are able to make their partner orgasm over 90% of the time.

219. If a man finds it hard to remain hard, it's best to avoid the girl being on top as gravity pulls the blood flow back from the penis.

220. Did you know that licorice reduces your libido? The licorice root has the ability to regulate cortisol levels in your body which in turn reduces your libido. High cortisol levels limit testosterone levels which causes your libido to down regulate.

221. 14% of women say they have had a "zone orgasm" which occurs when a part of the body is stimulated that aren't the boobs or vagina.

222. One in five men have admitted to watching porn at work.

223. Four out five people use contraceptives when losing their virginities.

224. There are over 100 million sexual intercourse encounters on our planet every single day.

225. Women who have a lot of sex have better control of their urination as the act tones the pelvic muscles that support the bowel, uterus, and bladder.

226. One in five women from the ages of twenty four to thirty four think that their sexual peak has passed while one in three men of the same age think the same thing.

227. The top three reasons for teenagers abstaining from sex is because they don't want to get pregnant, they haven't found the right person yet, and due to religion.

228. It takes three weeks of no orgasm for your testosterone levels to peak and boost your libido.

229. Only 14% of men surveyed said they let the woman take the lead while having sex.

230. One in ten couples use a vibrator or sex toy when in bed together.

231. 20% of men's penises are "show-ers" while 80% of them are "growers."

232. In Australia, one in five women have had sex with someone because they felt bad for them.

233. The lowest use of condom rates is found in adults over the age of forty.

234. Research conducted in 2005 showed that heavier women find men more attractive when they are hungry than after they've just had their meals.

235. Female video game players tend to have more sex and are happier in their relationships than women who don't play video games according to data from a Harris Interactive Survey.

236. The aroma of wine can arouse both men and women. The scents of many wines are believed to replicate human pheromones, the chemical substances that cause behavioral responses in humans.

237. Some women can be aroused by chimpanzee porn as a 2005 study published in Biological Psychology showed.

238. A 2010 study published in The Journal of Sexual Medicine found that between 20-30% of American men and women over the age of eighty remain sexually active.

239. Men over the age of sixty who pay for sex do so more often as they age.

240. Unfaithful men are more likely to die during sex than faithful ones.

241. Fetuses can get erections.

242. Upper Paleolithic art dating back 30,000 years depicts people using dildos to pleasure themselves and others. That means mankind invented sex toys long before the wheel.

243. The average man has eleven erections per day and nine erections a night.

244. The word "clitoris" is Greek for "divine and goddess like."

245. Throughout the United States, approximately 4% of the population self-identifies as gay, lesbian, or bisexual.

246. Married people are more likely to masturbate than people living alone.

247. Women who went to college are more likely to enjoy receiving and giving oral sex.

248. Formicophilia is the sexual interest of small insects or worms crawling over one's body.

249. Approximately 70% of people in the US admit to fantasizing about group sex at some point in their life, and more than 50% of those people actually follow through.

250. The creature named Funisia dorothea is thought by most scientists to be the first animal on the Earth to have sex, pushing back the history of sex by up to thirty million years.

251. Men who help with housework also tend to have more sex.

252. Approximately 1% of people worldwide identify themselves as a-sexual (having no strong sexual attraction to either sex).

253. Intercourse has also been called "afternoon delight," "dancing the mattress," "rumbusticating," "shtupping," "spearing the bearded clam," "horizontal refreshment," and "testing the mattress."

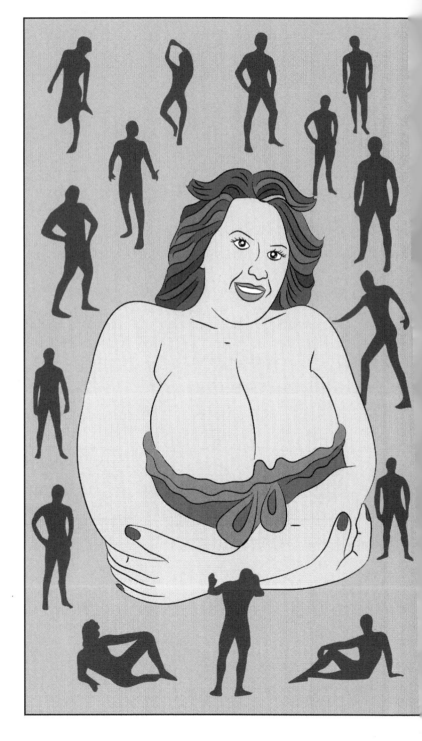

254. In 2004, Lisa Sparxx, a porn star, had intercourse with 919 men in twenty four hours, setting a new world record.

255. Couples in Greece have the most sex, approximately 164 times per year, and Brazil follows a close second with 145 times per year. The global average is 103.

256. The inventor of Kellogg's Corn Flakes, Dr. Kellogg, was an ardent anti-masturbation campaigner. He believed that a healthy diet would decrease a person's sexual thoughts.

257. The black widow spider eats her mate during or after sex. The hungry spider can eat as many as twenty lovers in one day.

258. The American Sociological Association found that the most mind-blowing sex typically comes when being in love with your partner.

259. Approximately 70% of men refuse to have sex during their girlfriend's period.

260. The most successful X-rated movie in history is "Deep Throat."

261. According to Pornhub, the kinkiest states are Wyoming, Alaska, Vermont, Virginia, and Oregon. California, surprisingly, is the least kinky.

267. A study that looked at the relationship between sexual orientation and orgasm occurrence found that heterosexual women climaxed 61.6% of the time, while homosexual women climaxed 74.7% of the time and bisexual women climaxed 58% of the time.

268. Sex hasn't always been associated with sin and guilt. Pre-Christian religions often regarded sex as a celebration and as a form of worship. Sex was seen as mirroring the sensual power of the Gods.

269. The left testicle usually hangs lower than the right for right-handed men. The opposite is true for lefties.

Bonus Facts !

According to one survey, 51% of respondents said they could go longer without sex than they could go without coffee.

People who sleep on their stomachs with their arms above their heads have more sexual dreams.

An apple a day can boost your sex life. According to one study, women who ate the fruit once a day had higher sexual quality of life.

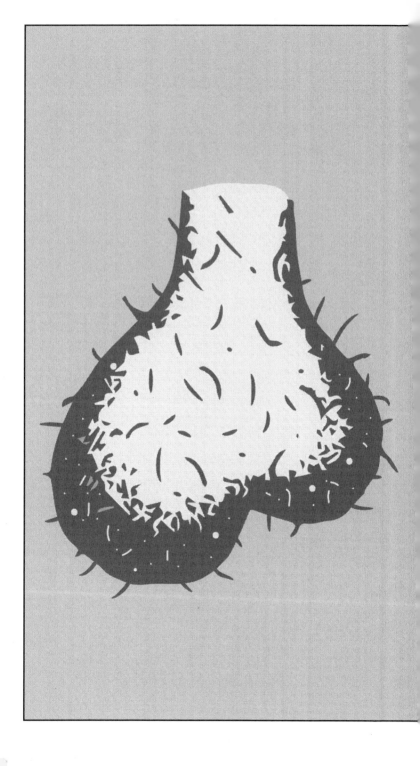

USEFUL TIPS PART II

262. Men who have sex three or more times a week have a lower chance of getting erectile dysfunction, as the act keep the package fit and healthy.

263. Women can excite a man even more when giving head by simply stroking the inside of their thighs. Since this area is near the genitals, the increased blood flow heightens the sensation. By also rubbing the side of the torso, you can stimulate a nerve that will make men more erect.

264. Approximately 500 to 1,000 people die due to asphyxiation in bed each year.

265. If your partner has a penis, a cock ring can really rev up something that's already good. By restricting blood flow to the penis, the ring makes their erection harder and stronger (also helpful if they have issues finishing too early or staying hard).

266. When experimenting with anal, anal foreplay is a must. Try giving or receiving a sacral massage; in other words, massaging the area just above the butt crack for fifteen to twenty minutes. It'll help release tension and loosen the whole area up.

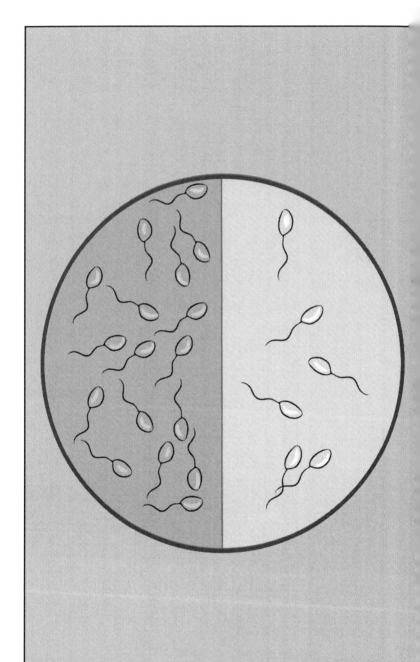

Straight men search for images of penises online almost as much as they do vaginas.

One out of every six Americans aged fourteen to forty nine has a genital herpes HSV-2 infection.

Penises used to have spines. They don't anymore because men have lost the DNA code that once made this possible.

There were penis curses in ancient Greece. In 2008, archeologists discovered a lead tablet on the island's south coast near Limassol. It reads: "May your penis hurt when you make love."

Straight men comprise more than half the audience for online transgender porn.

Ovulating women are more likely to cheat.

Male testosterone levels and sperm counts are only a quarter of what they were a century ago.

Educated white women have more anal sex than any other group.

Gay men have bigger penises than straight men.

Woman on top provides easier access to the vulva and clitoris than in other positions meaning more chance of the girl climaxing.

The most common cause of penile rupture is vigorous masturbation.

The states where couples have the shortest lovemaking sessions are Alaska (1:21), South Dakota (1:30), Montana (2:03) and Georgia. The states where couples have the longest love making sessions are New Mexico (7:01), West Virginia (5:38), Idaho (5:11), South Carolina (4:48), and Missouri (4:22).

Although nearly any body part or item of clothing may be an object of sexual fetishism, the shoe and the foot are the two most common fetishes in Western society.

Three quarters of all men think that it's harmful to not have sex.

Cardrona bra fence is a controversial tourist attraction located in Central Otago, New Zealand. Long ago, people driving by started to add bras to a rural fence; it eventually became covered in hundreds of ladies bras.

Printed in Great Britain
by Amazon